Reading STREET

Grade **K**

Scott Foresman
Take-Home
Decodable Readers

PEARSON
Scott Foresman

Editorial Offices: Glenview, Illinois • Parsippany, New Jersey • New York, New York
Sales Offices: Boston, Massachusetts • Duluth, Georgia • Glenview, Illinois
Coppell, Texas • Sacramento, California • Mesa, Arizona

ISBN: 0-328-16873-4

9 10 V084 14 13 12 11 10 09 08

Contents

Who Am I?

Written by Bob Atkins

Illustrated by Yvette Pierre

Skills

Word Recognition

I   am

Letter Recognition

Aa   Bb   Cc   Dd   Ee

I am Dad.

8

I am Ann.

I am Emma.

I am Ben.

I am Ed.

4

I am Cam.

© Pearson Education, Inc.

I am Dot.

5

Am I?

Written by George Helm

Illustrated by Tori Wheaton

Skills

Word Recognition

I   am

Letter Recognition

Ff   Gg   Hh   Ii   Jj   Kk   Ll

I am Gus.

8

I am Jan.

Am I Hanna?

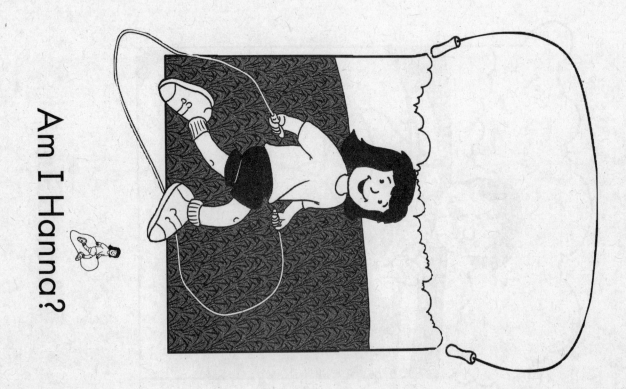

Am I Fran?

I am Kim.

4

I am Len.

Am I Ken?

The Little Toys

Written by Roger Jons
Illustrated by Scott Salinski

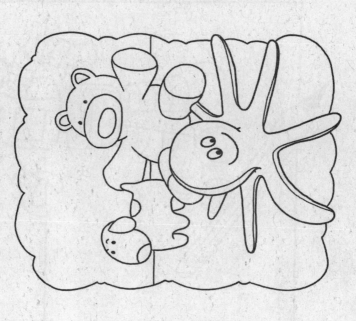

Skills

Word Recognition

I	the	little
	am	

Letter Recognition

Mm	Nn	Oo	Pp	Qq	Rr	Ss

I am the little spaceship.

8

I am the little robot.

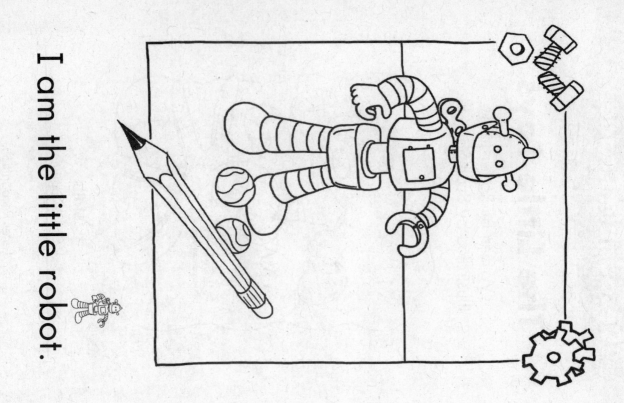

I am the little block.

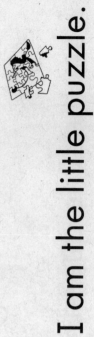

I am the little puzzle.

I am the little train.

4

I am the little queen.

I am the little octopus.

5

At the Zoo

Written by Nitty Jones

Illustrated by Amy Sparks

Skills

Word Recognition

I   am   the   little

Letter Recognition

Tt   Uu   Vv   Ww   Xx   Yy   Zz

I am the little umbrella bird.

8

2

I am the little walrus.

I am the little zebra.

7

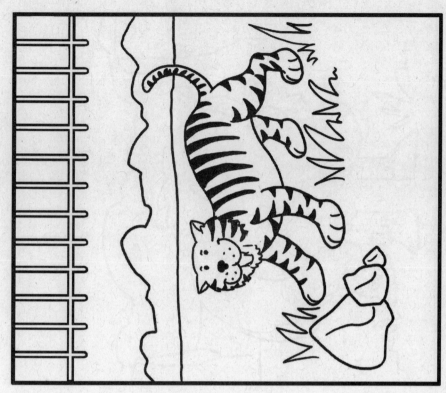

I am the little tiger.

I am the little rhino.

6

4

I am the little yak.

I am the little ox.

5

Animal Friends

Written by Phil Morton

Illustrated by Julie Wordman

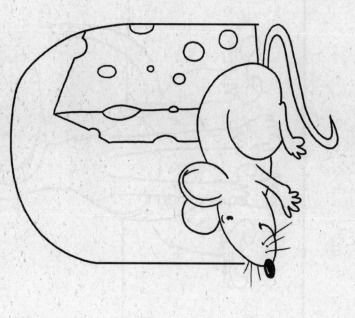

Skills

Word Recognition

I   am   a   little

Letter Recognition

Consonant Mm /m/

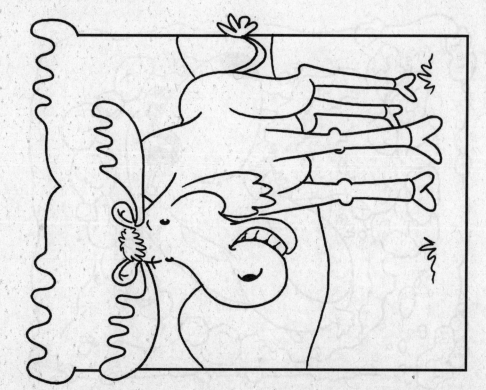

I am a little moose.
Am I little?

8

I am a little monkey.

I am a little mole.

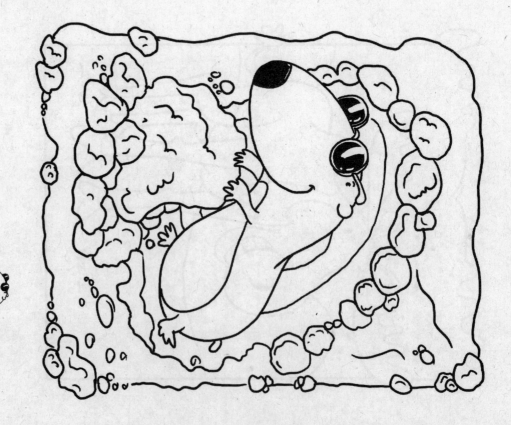

I am a little mule.

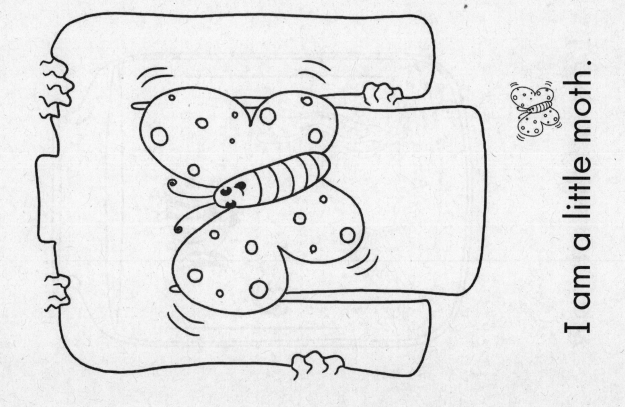

I am a little moth.

I am a little mouse.

I am a little minnow.

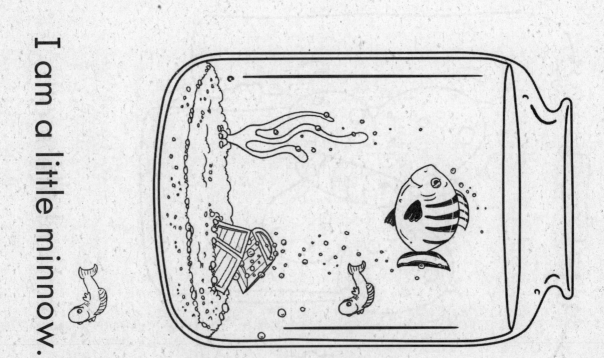

Let's Go

Written by Liz Cristie

Illustrated by Larry Jordon

Skills

Word Recognition

I   to   a

Letter Recognition

Consonant Tt /t/

I walk home.

I walk to a tiger.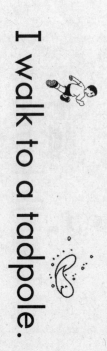

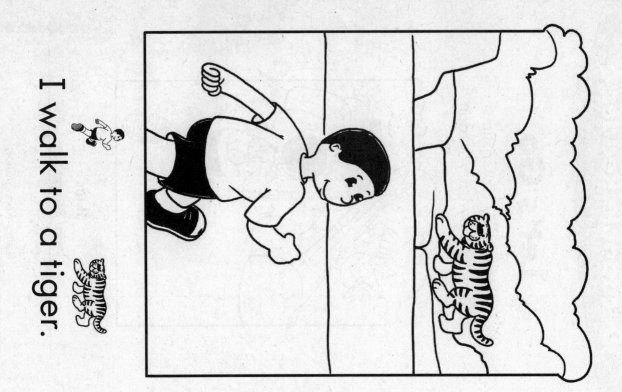

I walk to a tadpole.

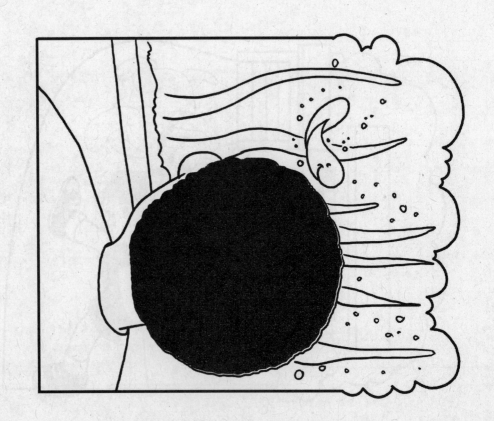

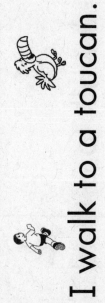

I walk to a toucan.

I walk to a turtle.

4

I walk to a turkey.

I walk to a toad.

5

Decodable Reader 7

A Little Mat

Written by Alex Altman

Illustrated by Mary Stern

Phonics Skill

Short a

am   Tam   mat   at

Tam is at the mat.

8

2

I am Tam.

The mat is little.

7

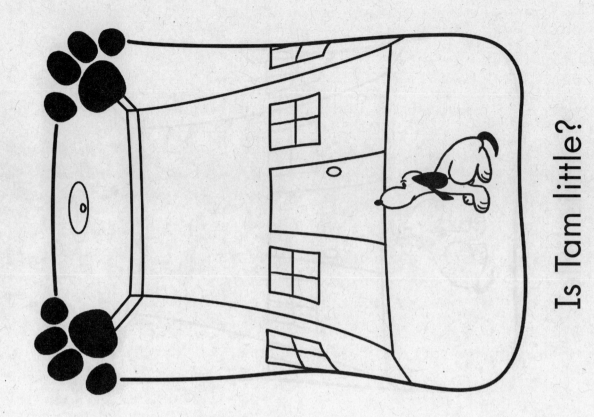

Is Tam little?

Is the mat little?

Tam is little.

I have a mat.

Sam and Tam

Written by Paul Thomas

Illustrated by Katie Snell

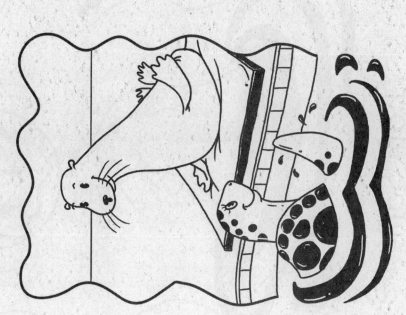

Phonics Skill

Consonant Ss /s/

Sam   sat

Tam sat.
Sam sat.

8

2

I am Sam.

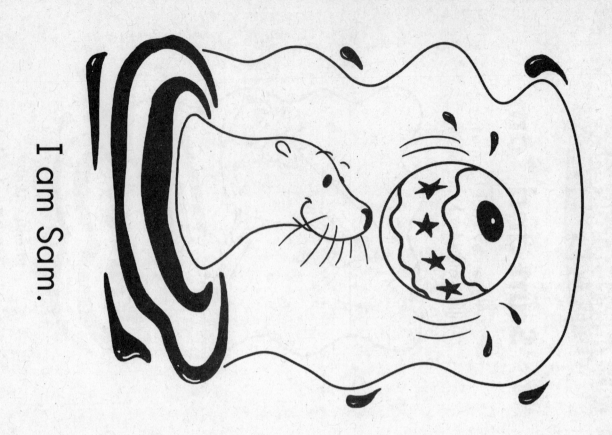

Tam sat at the mat.

7

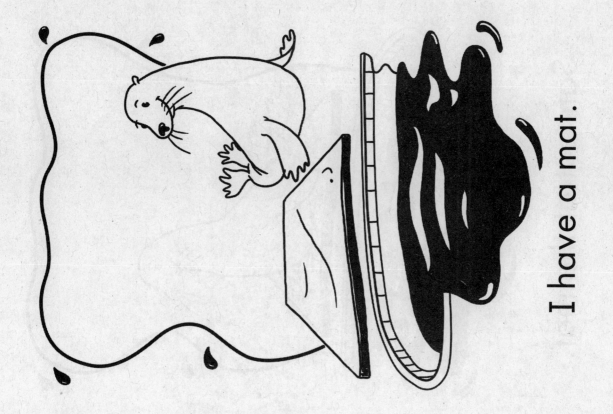

I have a mat.

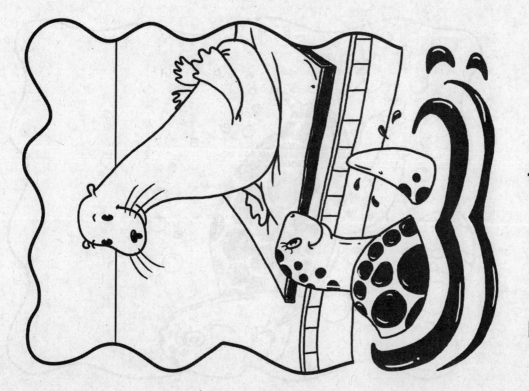

Tam is at the mat.

Sam sat at the mat.

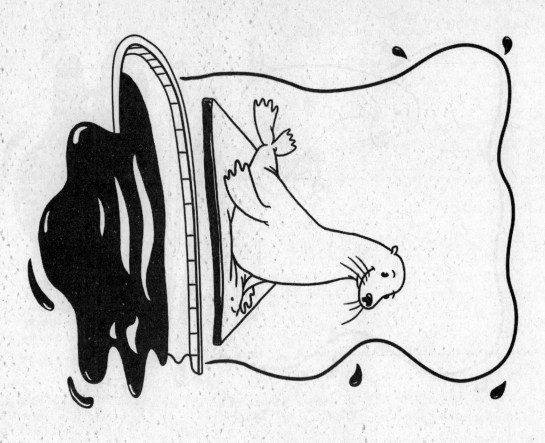

I am Tam.

My Map

Written by Jerry Moore

Illustrated by Chris Brown

Phonics Skill

Consonant Pp /p/

Pam   map   tap   pat

We like the map.

8

I am Pam.

We pat at the map.

I have a map.

We tap the map.

The map sat at the mat.

4

I tap my map.

5

My Cap

Written by Sue Bear
Illustrated by Lori Burk

Phonics Skill
Consonant Cc /k/

Cam   Mac   cap

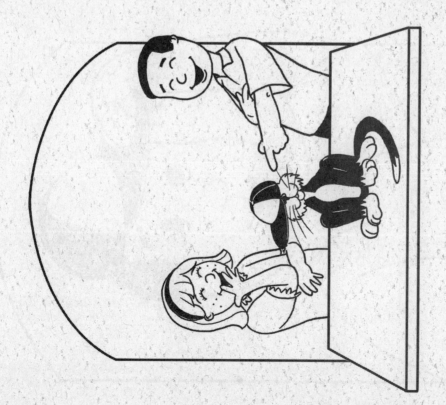

I like my cap.

8

I am Cam.
I am Mac.

Is the cap my cap?

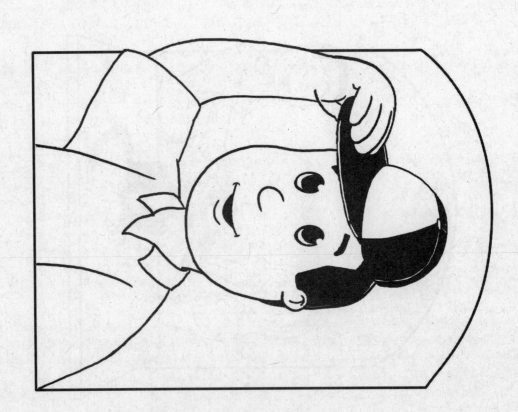

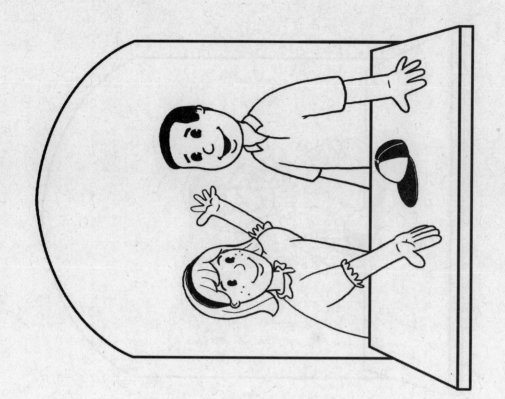

We have a cap.

Mac is at the cap.

4

Cam is at the cap.

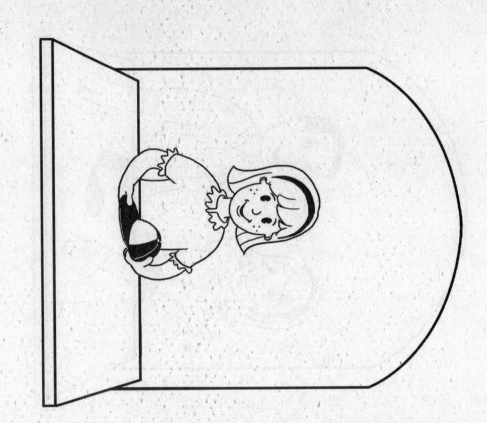

Is the cap my cap?

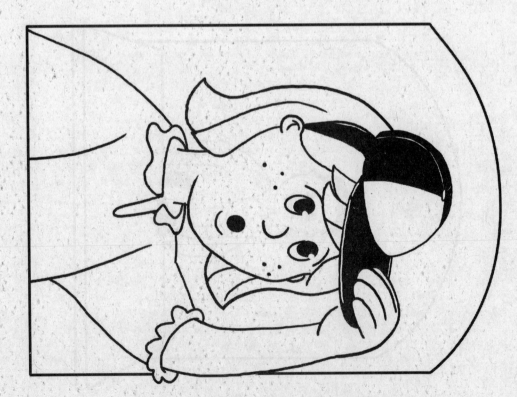

5

Tip and Pat

Written by Kate Brand
Illustrated by Carl Johnson

Phonics Skill
Short i

Tip   it   sit

Sit, Tip, sit.
Sit, Pat, sit.

Tip is a cat.

It is for Pat.

He is my cat.

It is for Tip.

4

Pat is a cat.

He is my cat.

5

Tim and Sam

Written by Joei Shavitz
Illustrated by Lawrence Paul

Phonics Skill
Short i

sit	Tim	tip	it

It is a mat for Tim.

8

I am Sam.
I sit.

I am Sam.
I sit.

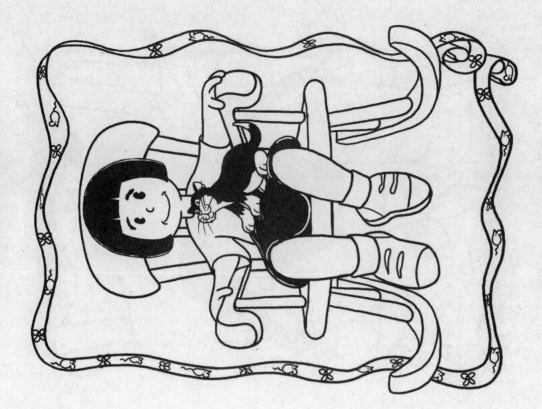

Tim sat.
I have Tim.

We tip.

4

He is my cat.

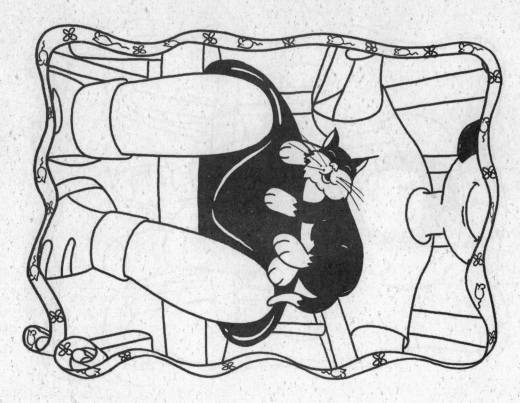

I pat Tim.

5

Nat!

Written by Patricia Crotty
Illustrated by Dan Vick

TAP
TAP
TAP

Phonics Skills

Consonant Bb /b/ | Consonant Nn /n/

bat

can
Nat
Nan

Nat can bat!

8

Can Nat bat it?
Nat can bat it.

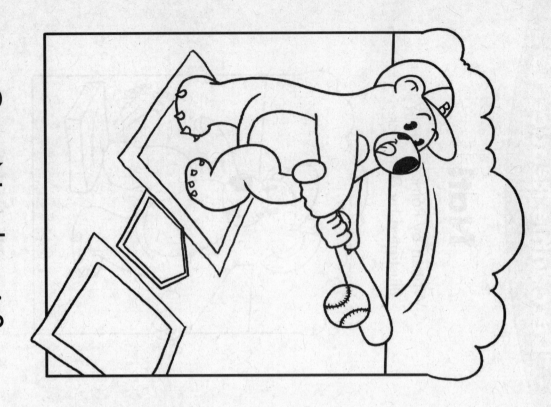

Nat sat with me.

Can Nat tap it?
Nat can tap it.

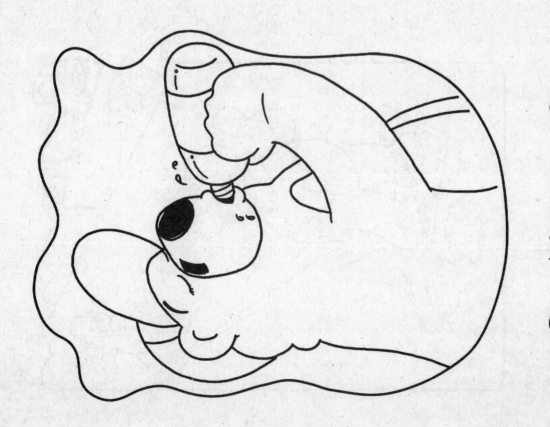

3

Can Nat sip it?
Nat can sip it.

4

Can Nat pat it?
Nat can pat it.

Nan can bat it.
She can bat.

5

Rip with Rap

Written by Peggy Lee
Illustrated by Lucy Smythe

Phonics Skill
Consonant Rr /r/

Rip   rat   ran   Rap

Rip can nap.
Rap can bat.

8

Rip the rat can sit.

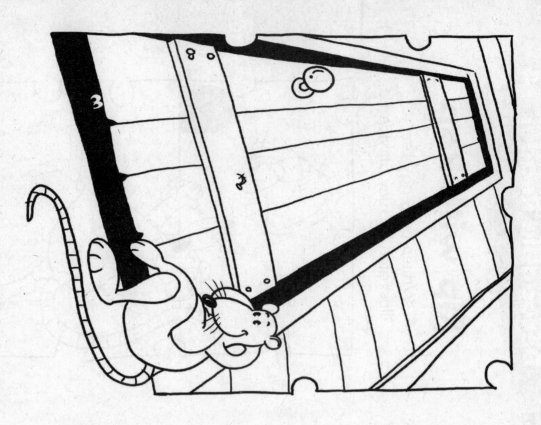

Rip is with me.
Rip can sit.

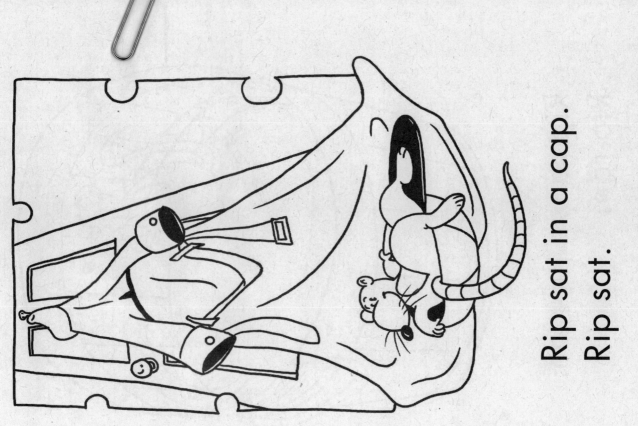

Rip sat in a cap.
Rip sat.

Rip can bat the cap.
She can bat it.

4

Rip ran in the can.
Rip ran.

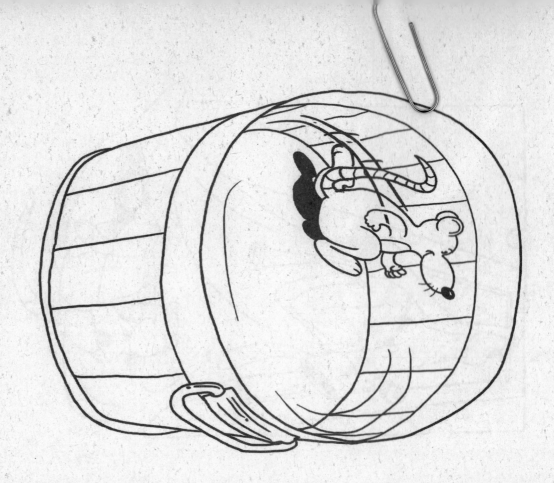

Rip sat in the can.
Rip sat.

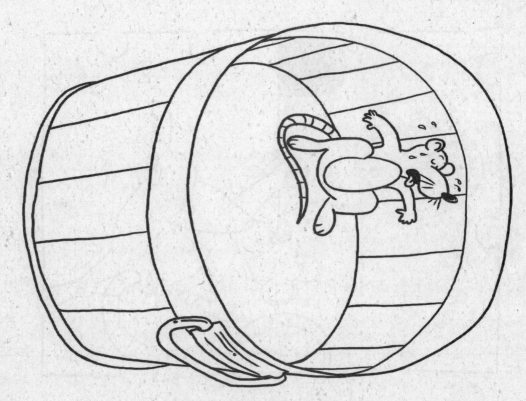

5

Dad Did

Written by June Harper
Illustrated by Bethany Mills

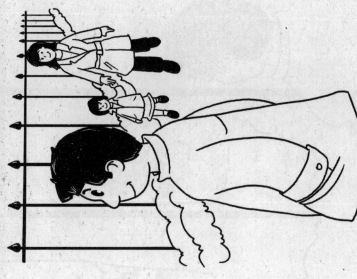

Phonics Skills

Consonant Dd /d/	Consonant Kk /k/
did	kid
Dad	

Dad can.
Dad did.

8

Did Dad see the cat?
Dad did.

Did Dad look at it?
Dad did.

Did Dad look at it?
Dad did.

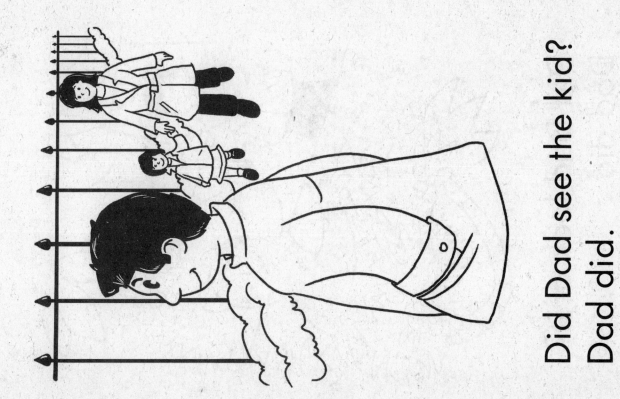

Did Dad see the kid?
Dad did.

4

Did Dad see the rat?
Dad did.

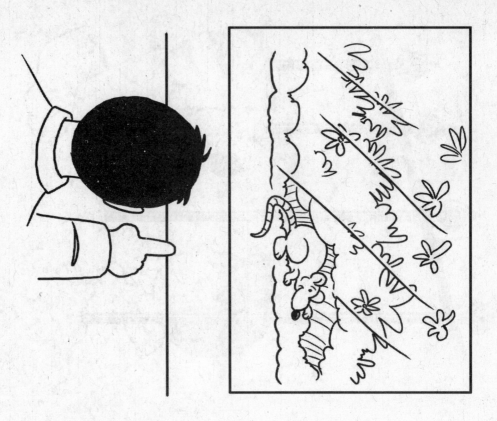

Did Dad look at it?
Dad did.

In the Kit!

Written by Leon Cross

Illustrated by Jeff Blake

Phonics Skill
Consonant Ff /f/

fan   fat   fit

Kip can fit it in the kit.

8

Kip can see a kit.

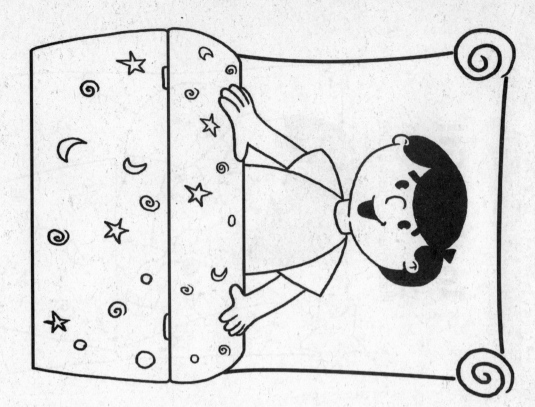

Kip can pat.
Pat, Kip, pat.

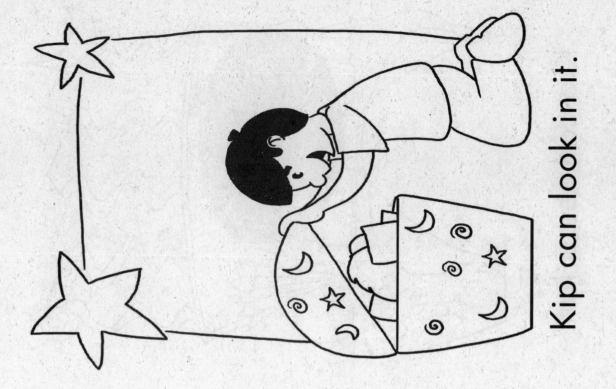

Kip can look in it.

Kip can see a fat cat.

4

Kip can see a fan.

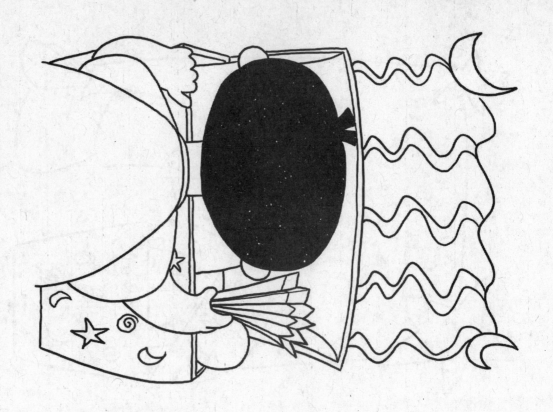

Kip can fan.
Fan, Kip, fan.

5

The Mop

Written by Donald Newman
Illustrated by Marcia Geller

Phonics Skill
Short o

Tom	mop	cot	on	Dot	top

They look at the mop.
Can you mop?

8

Can Tom mop?
Tom can mop.

Pat can fit on
top of the cot.

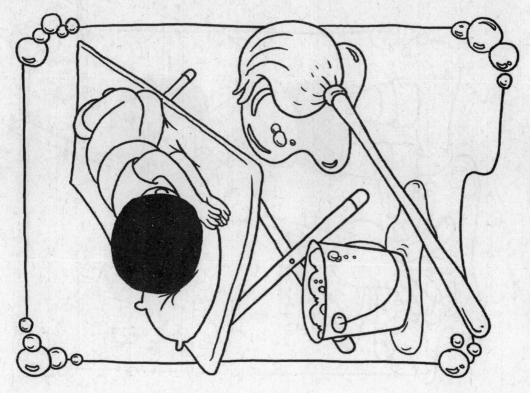

Tom can nap on
top of the cot.

Can Pat mop?
Pat can mop.

4

Can Dot mop?
Dot can mop.

Dot can sit on
top of the cot.

5

Tip the Top

Written by Page Kuhl

Illustrated by David Muntz

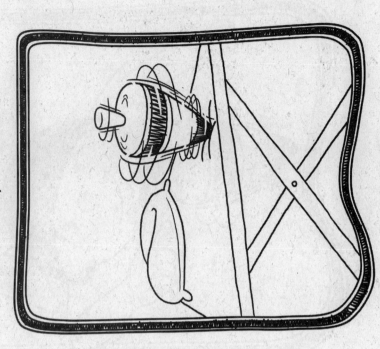

Phonics Skill

Short o

top	Don	not	on
cot	Dot	Rod	

It can not tip!

8

2

Rod can pat it.
Rod can tip the top.

They can pat the top.
They can tip it.

7

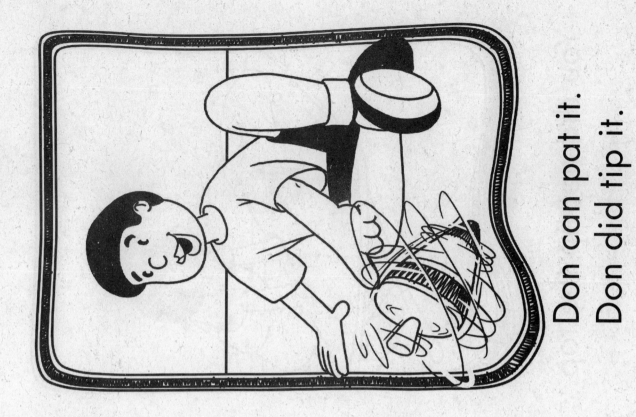

Don can pat it.
Don did tip it.

Dot did not tip it.

4

You did not tip the top.

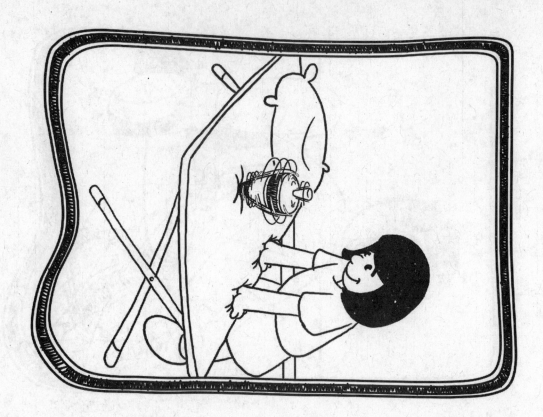

© Pearson Education, Inc.

It is on top of the cot.

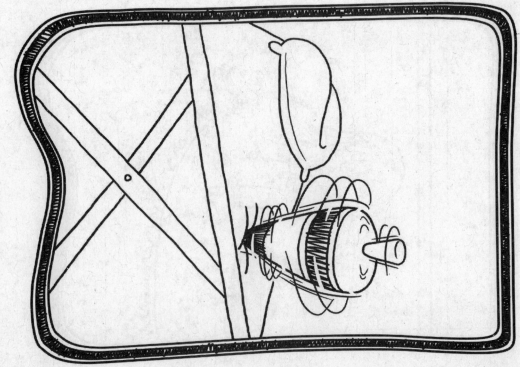

5

Hob Can Hit

Written by Roy Kass

Illustrated by Ryan Bines

Phonics Skill

Consonant Hh /h/

Hob	hit	hot
hat	had	

Pop! Hob hit it!
Hob did it!
They are not sad.

8

2

That man is Dan Hob.
Hob can hit.
Hob can do it!

Hob is hot.
Hob had a big hat.

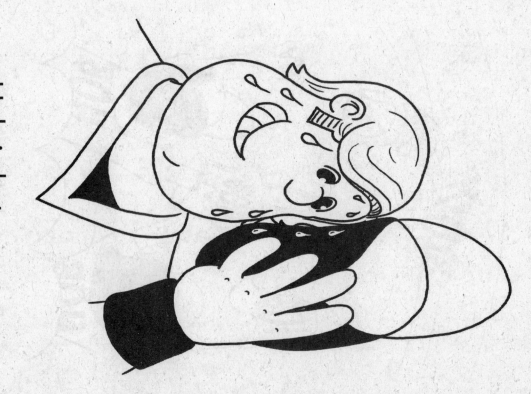

7

That fan is Pam.
Can Pam see Hob?
Pam can.

Did Hob hit it?
Hob did not.

That fan is Sam.
Can Sam see Hob?
Sam can.

Did Hob hit it?
Hob did not.

Can It Fit?

Written by Myleen Rush

Illustrated by Gloria Leek

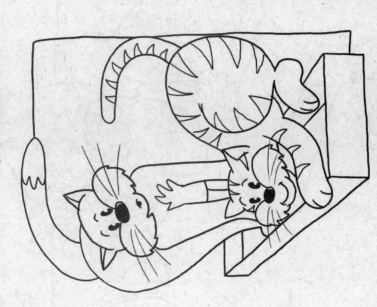

Phonics Skill

Consonant Ll /l/

| Lil | lid | lap |
| lit | doll | |

They are on Lil.

8

Tab sat on a lap.
Kit did not.

Can Tab fit on Lil?
Can Kit fit on Lil?

Lil lit it.
Do you see Tab?

They fit in that lid.

4

Lil had a doll.
Kit can bat it.

Kit sat in the lid.
Can Tab fit?

5

One to Five

Written by Heather Leavy
Illustrated by Kris Pool

Phonics Skill
Consonant Blends

flop	spin	slam	drop
plop	land	jump	stop

Stop! Stop! Stop!

8

One sat on a mat.
Flop!

Flop! Spin! Slam! Drop! Plop!

Two ran on a pan.
Spin! Spin!

Five jump on top.
Plop! Plop! Plop! Plop!

4

Three hid in a lid.
Slam! Slam! Slam!

Four land on a lap.
Drop! Drop! Drop!

5

Gil Got One

Written by William Dillberts

Illustrated by Hillary Gem

Gil is not sad.

8

Gil got one.
Pop!
Sad Gil.

Mom had a plan.
Mom got Gil a flag.

Gil got two.
Pop! Pop!
Sad Gil.

Gil got five.
Pop! Pop! Pop! Pop!
Sad Gil.

4

Gil got three.
Pop! Pop! Pop!
Sad Gil.

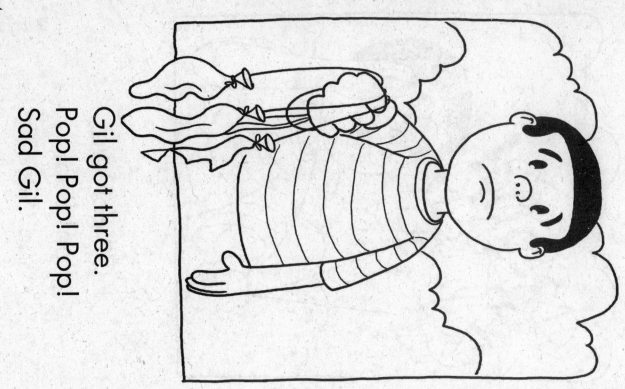

Gil got four.
Pop! Pop! Pop! Pop!
Sad Gil.

5

Red Hen

Written by Nathan Aguilera

Illustrated by Samantha Johnson

Phonics Skill

Short e

| get | Red | Hen | Ben |
| pen | Ken | Len | |

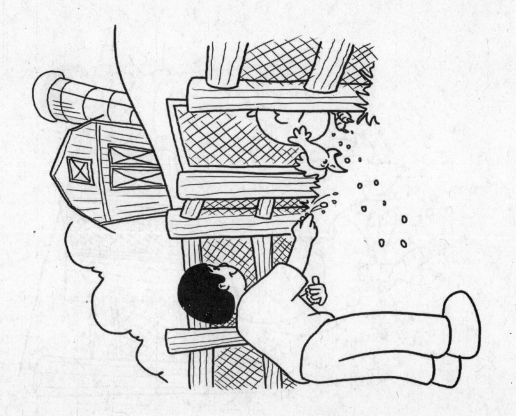

Len got Red Hen!

8

2

Get Red Hen, Ben.
Red Hen can go in the pen.

Red Hen did not get in the pen.

7

Red Hen ran from Ben.
Red Hen hid here.

Red Hen ran from Ken.
Red Hen hid here.

Red Hen did not get in the pen.

4

Get Red Hen, Ken.
Red Hen can go in the pen.

5

A Pet Hen

Written by Fran Quinn

Illustrated by Jason Edwards

Phonics Skill

Short e

Peg	met	Ned	pet
Hen	pen	bed	get
fed	let		

Peg got in bed.
Let Peg nap, Hen.

8

Peg met Ned.
Peg got a pet from Ned.
Here is Hen.

Peg fed Hen.

Did Hen have a pen?
Hen did not.

Peg got Hen a bed.
Get in, Hen.

4

Peg got Hen a pen.
Go in, Hen.

Did Hen have a bed?
Hen did not.

5

On a Jet

Written by Mike O'Hern
Illustrated by Joan Tortle

Phonics Skills

Consonant Ww /w/	Consonant Jj /j/
Wes	job
wet	jet
will	Jen

Wes met Jen.
Wes and Jen grin.

8

2

Wes had a big job.
Wes got the yellow jet wet.

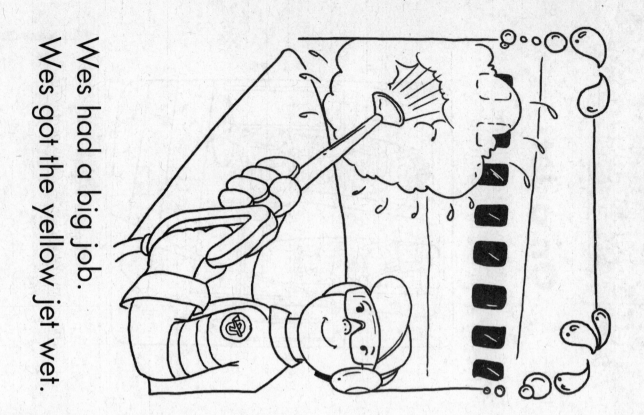

Wes had a big grin.
It can go fast.

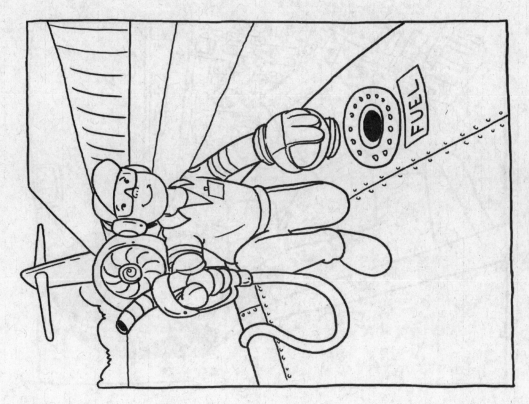

Wes will fill it.
Wes will fill it with gas.

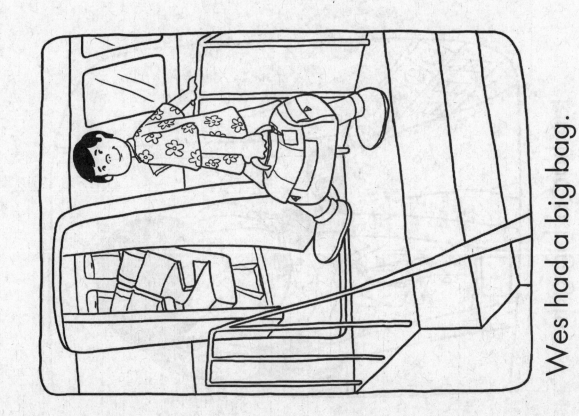

Wes had a big bag.
Wes got in the green jet.

Jen had a big job.
Jen sat in the blue jet.

Jen had a big grin.
Jen can hop in.
It can go fast.

Fox Can Fix It!

Written by Roger Bines

Illustrated by Chris Lemon

Phonics Skill

Consonant Xx /ks/

| Fox | fix | box | Ox |

Fox sat.
Fox can fix it!

Pig had a blue and yellow cap.
It had a rip in it.
Get it to Fox. Fox can fix it.

2

Did Fox fix it?
Fox did.

7

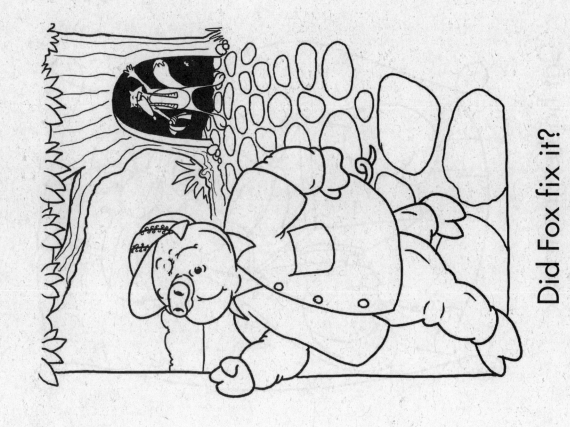

Did Fox fix it?
Fox did!

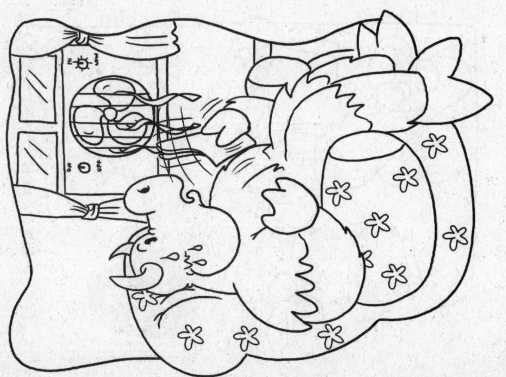

Ox is hot.
The fan is not on.
Get it to Fox. Fox can fix it.

4

Cat had a green box.
It did not have a top.
Get it to Fox. Fox can fix it.

Did Fox fix it?
Fox did!

5

Fun for Bud

Written by Judy Wienhouse

Illustrated by Gabrial Peterson

Phonics Skill

Short u

Bud	pup	up	ruff	run	jump
sun	dug	mud	fun	tub	hug

Bud can get a big hug.
Bud can get in bed.

8

2

Bud is a pup.
Bud sat up.
Bud said, "Ruff, ruff."

Get Bud in the tub.
Get Bud wet.

7

What did Bud see?
Run, Bud, run.

Bud dug in mud.
Bud had fun.

4

Bud can run fast.
Bud can jump up.

Bud sat in the sun.
It was hot.
Bud got wet.

5

Jan at the Fair

Written by Josh Dart

Illustrated by Dave Goodman

Phonics Skill

Short u

bus	sub	drum	bug
fun	cup	mud	tub

Jan can get on the bus.
Jan had fun!

8

2

Jan sat on the bus.
What will Jan do?

Jan can drop mud in a tub.
Jan will get it in.

7

"Can I get in the sub?" said Jan.
Jan will get in.

Jan can sip.
The red cup was big.

4

Jan can hit the drum.
Jan will grin.

Jan can hop on the bug.
Jan will have fun.

5

Zip Up, Val!

Written by Susan Whit

Illustrated by Kevin Kessler

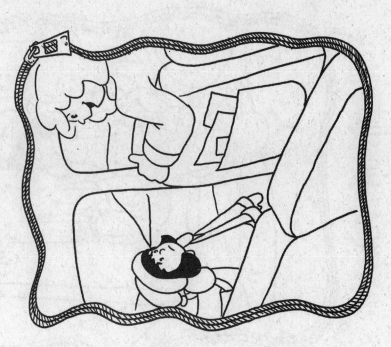

Phonics Skills

Consonant Vv /v/	Consonant Zz /z/
Val	zip

Come here, Val.
Do not zip up, Val.
It is hot!

2

Zip up, Val.
It is not hot.
Val ran.

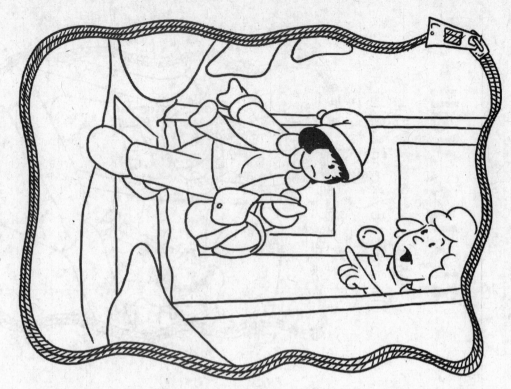

Val got on a jet.
Val got on a jet with Dad.

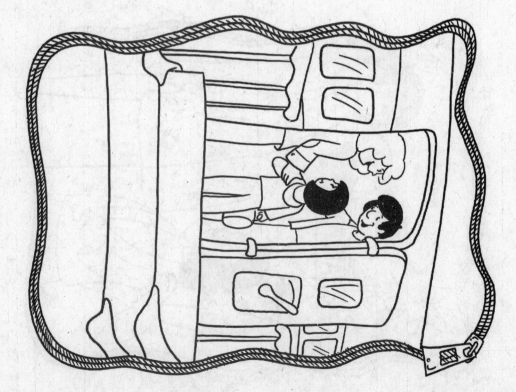

7

Val got in it.
Zip up, Val.
It is not hot.

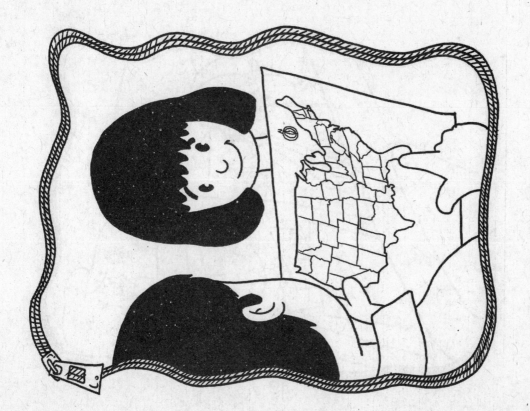

Where is it hot?
Dad had a map.
It can get hot here.

4

Zip up, Val.
It is not hot.
Val ran.

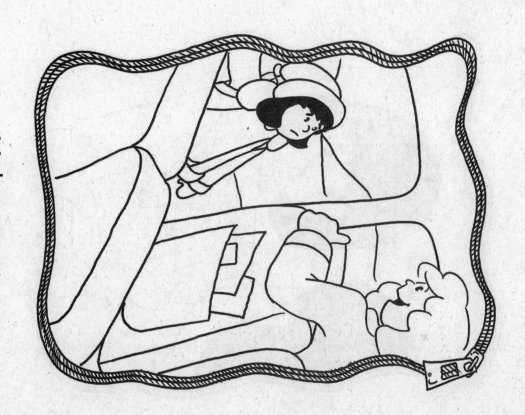

Val got in it.
Zip up, Val.
It is not hot.

5

The Quiz

Written by Cathy Collins
Illustrated by Eric Mendez

Phonics Skills

Consonant Yy /y/	Consonant Qq /kw/
yes	quiz
yak	quit

Jim got the quiz.
Can Jim pass?
Yes, Jim did!

8

2

Jim will get a quiz.
Jim and Mom come in.
Jim and Mom sit.

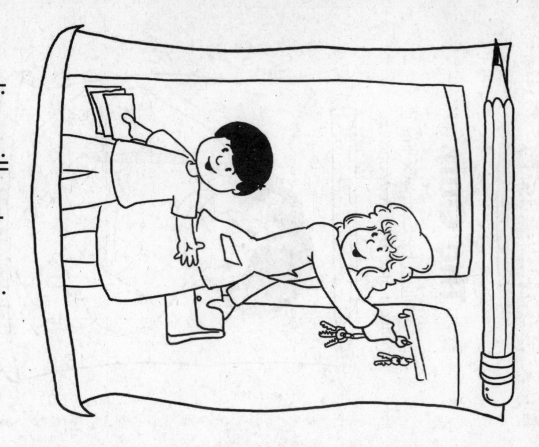

Jim will quit.
Jim will run fast.
Jim will get on the bus.

7

Can Mom help Jim?
Yes, Mom can help him.
Jim sat. Mom sat.

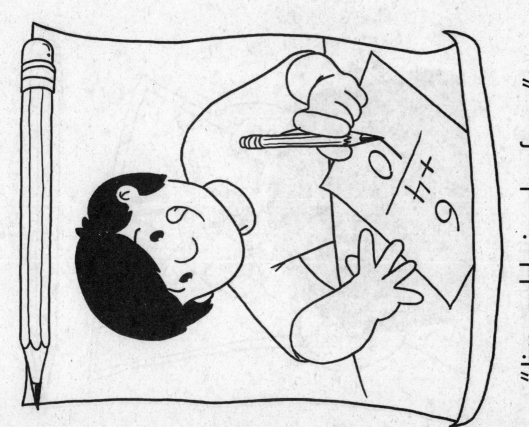

"Jim, add six plus four."
Jim sat.
Six plus four is ten.

4

"Jim, is a yak an ox?"
Jim sat. Jim said,
"A yak is not an ox."

"Jim, where is the big yak?"
Jim sat. Jim said,
"The big yak is on top."

YAK

5

If Kip Can

Written by Sara Blumenthal

Illustrated by Ken Ye

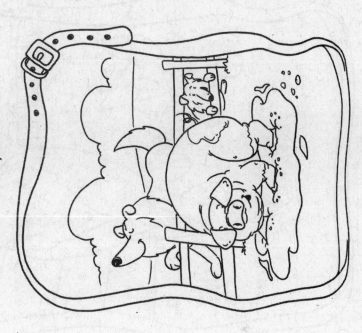

Phonics Skills

Short a		Short i		
can	tap	Kip	big	will
pass	gap	dig	if	Pig
Sam		fit	in	
Cat				
nap				

Sam can do what Kip can do!

8

2

Kip is big.
Sam is little.
Sam will go with Kip.

If Kip can nap,
Sam can nap.
Kip can nap. Will Sam nap?

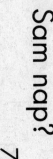

7

If Kip can dig here,
Sam can dig here.
Kip can dig. Will Sam dig?

If Kip can fit in the gap,
Sam can fit in the gap.
Kip can fit. Will Sam fit?

If Kip can tap Cat,
Sam can tap Cat.
Kip can tap Cat. Will Sam tap?

4

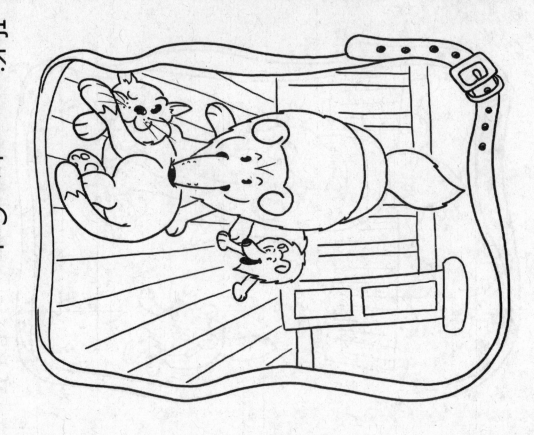

If Kip can pass Pig,
Sam can pass Pig.
Kip can pass Pig. Will Sam pass?

5

Will Cass Come?

Written by Tracy Hawks

Illustrated by Bill Pars

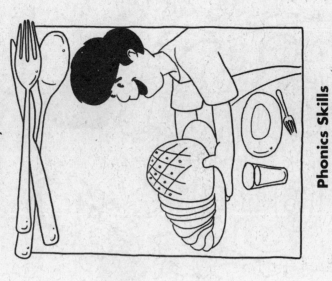

Phonics Skills

Short a	Short i		Short o	
Ann	sit	Kim	Tom	Jon
sad	did	will	got	not
pan	miss	it	hot	pot
can	big	in		
jam	fix	mix		
Cass	dip	fill		
ham	grin	sit		
pass				
yam				
tan				

It is Cass!

Cass can grin.

Cass can sit with us.

8

2

Sit, Tom. Sit, Kim.
Sit, Ann. Sit, Jon.

Kim can come with red jam.
Jam is in a tan pot.
Pass us red jam, Kim.

7

Where did Cass go?
Cass will miss it.
Cass is sad.

Jon can mix dip.
Dip will fill that pan.
Pass us dip, Jon.

4

Tom got a big ham.
Ham is in a big pan.
Pass us ham, Tom.

Ann can fix a yam.
It is not hot.
Pass us the yam, Ann.

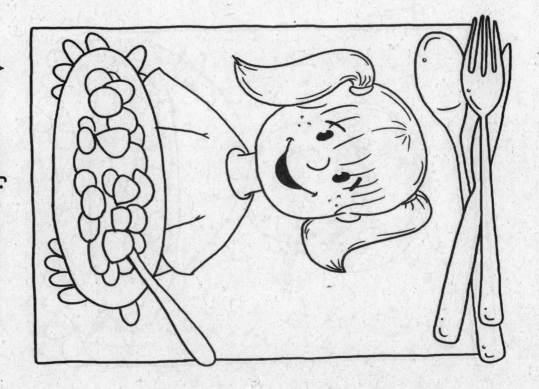

5

The Red Egg

Written by Robert Smith
Illustrated by Perry Scott

Phonics Skills

Short a	Short e		Short i	Short o
mat	Ed	red	big	got
sat	hen	egg	in	on
can	set	bed	it	hop
pass	well	net	tin	toss
add			Tim	pot
ham			grin	
and				

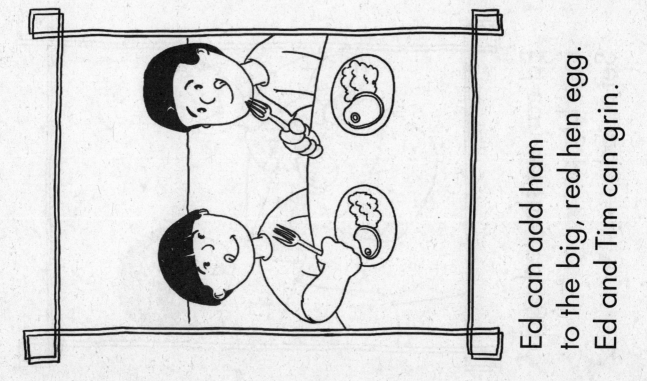

Ed can add ham
to the big, red hen egg.
Ed and Tim can grin.

8

2

Ed got a big,
red hen egg.
Ed set the egg on a mat.

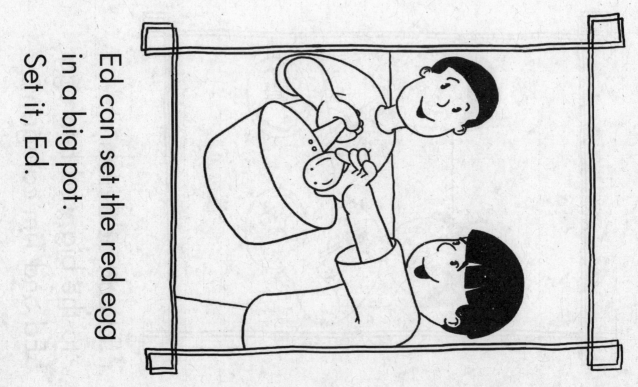

Ed can set the red egg
in a big pot.
Set it, Ed.

7

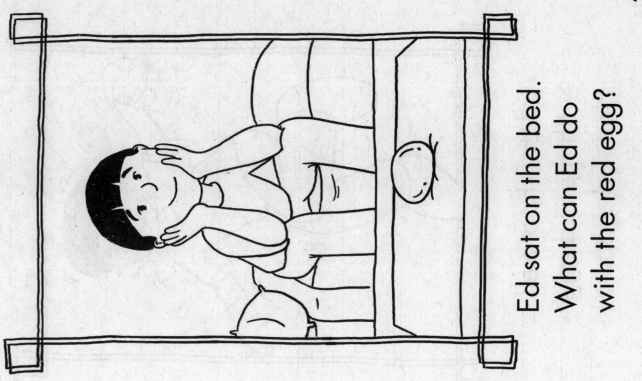

Ed sat on the bed.
What can Ed do
with the red egg?

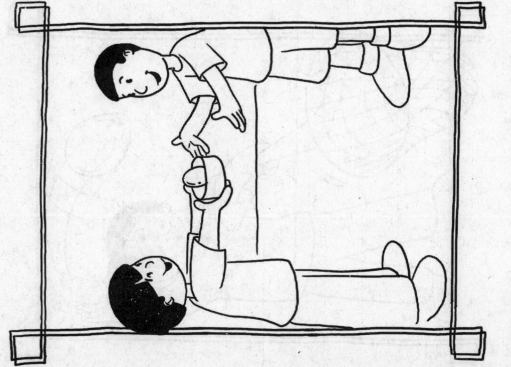

Ed can pass the red egg
in a tin can.
Pass it, Ed.

4

Ed can hop well
with the red egg.
Hop, Ed, hop.

Ed can toss the red egg
in a big net.
Toss it, Ed.

5

Fun with Spot

Written by Cassandra Belton

Illustrated by Joseph Green

SPOT

Phonics Skills

Short a			Short e	Short i		
can	fast	lap	pet	big	will	hill
had				dig	in	did
				sip	if	it
				sit		

Short o			Short u		
Spot	not	lot	pup	run	fun
hot	on	top	up	mud	tug
			hug	jump	

I will hug Spot.
Spot had fun.
We will jump up.

2

Spot is my pup.
Spot is not a big pet.

Spot can sit.
Spot will sit on my lap
on top of the hill.

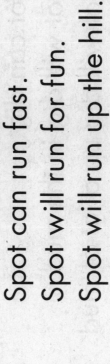

Spot can run fast.
Spot will run for fun.
Spot will run up the hill.

Spot can sip.
If it is hot,
Spot will sip a lot.

Spot can dig.
Spot will dig in the mud.
Spot will dig up a lot of mud.

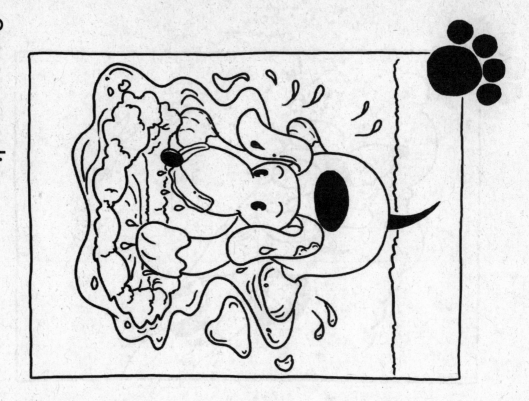

Spot can tug.
I will tug with Spot.
What did Spot tug?

Fun in the Sun

Written by Harry Reynolds

Illustrated by Dan Vick

Phonics Skills

Short a			Short e			Short i		
Jan	tan	had	red	net	wet	will	in	big
fat	an	bat	Deb	fed	Wes	pig	Kim	slim
can			hen	fell	egg	mitt	win	did
			well			quit		

Short o			Short u		
Todd	got	hot	fun	sun	mud
not	Rob		snug	run	

They had fun in the hot sun!

2

Todd got a red net.
Jan got a tan net.
Will they have fun?

Kim can run well. Kim did win.
Rob did not quit. Rob did win.

7

Todd got wet.
Jan got wet.
They had fun in the hot sun!

Kim got a slim bat.
Rob got a snug mitt.
Will they win?

4

Deb fed a big, fat pig.
Wes fed a red hen.
Will they have fun?

Deb fell in the mud.
Wes got an egg.
They had fun in the hot sun!

5

The Box

Written by Andrea Brooks

Illustrated by Linda Bird

Phonics Skills

Short a		Short e		Short i	
an	Pam Cat	yes	let bed	big	did in
can	had tan	red	fed	it	sit
fan	flat pan				
ham	bad				

Short u		
jump	yum fun	

Short o		
odd	box Tom	
Fox	on hot	
not		

"Not bad for an odd, big box," Pam Cat said.

8

2

"What an odd, big box!"
Pam Cat said.
"Can I see?"

Pam Cat had hot ham
with Tom Fox.
Yum, yum! They had fun.

7

"Yes, you can," said Tom Fox.
Tom Fox did let Pam Cat
see in the box.

Tom Fox had a flat pan
in the big box.
Tom Fox fed Pam Cat hot ham.

4

Tom Fox had a tan bed
in the big box.
Tom Fox can jump on it.

Tom Fox had a red fan
in the big box.
Tom Fox can sit with the fan on.

5